Little Scientists ®

A "hands-on" approach to learning

Exploring Light and Color

Dear Parents,

Young children are natural scientists, curious about the
world around them. They have an infinite capacity to learn
and are eager to know why and how things work the way
they do. Little Scientists, Hands-On Activities begins with
the simple questions most children ask and then shows them
how to explore and find out for themselves. Our acclaimed
Little Scientists, "hands-on" approach instills in children a
passion for the exciting world of science and helps children
develop specific scientific skills that will provide a strong
foundation for later learning.

With this book, you can join me on a journey into the
wonders of Water and Bubbles. Together we will discover
the unlocked secrets of water and learn how to create bubbles,
clouds, and many other exciting things.

Your Little Scientist can email me at
Dr_Heidi@Little-Scientists.com

Wishing you success,

Dr. Heidi

Little Scientists®
A "hands-on" approach to learning

Exploring
Light and Color

Heidi Gold-Dworkin, Ph.D.

McGraw-Hill
New York   San Francisco   Washington, D.C.
Auckland   Bogotá   Caracas   Lisbon   London   Madrid   Mexico City
Milan   Montreal   New Delhi   San Juan   Singapore   Sydney   Tokyo   Toronto

This book is dedicated to my children
Aviva, Olivia, and Robert

This book would not have been possible
without the contributions from the following
staff members at Little Scientists:®

June Stevens

Melissa Dailey

Meredith Girard

Bec Luty

Larry Russick

Linda Burian

Avi Ornstein

McGraw-Hill

A Division of The **McGraw-Hill** Companies

pbk   2 3 4 5 6 7 8 9 0 QPD / QPD   0 9 8 7 6 5 4 3 2 1

ISBN 0-07-134821-2

Library of Congress Cataloging-in-Publication data applied for.

McGraw-Hill books are available at special quantity discounts to use as premiums and sales promotions. For more information, please write to the Director of Special Sales, McGraw-Hill, 11 West 19th Street, New York, NY 10011. Or contact your local bookstore.

Acquisitions editor: Mary Loebig Giles
Senior editing supervisor: Patricia V. Amoroso
Senior production supervisor: Clare B. Stanley
Left page illustrations: Robert K. Ullman <r.k.ullman@worldnet.att.net>
Right page illustrations: K. Almadingen <dzbersin@aol.com>
Book design: Jaclyn J. Boone <bookdesign@rcn.com>

 Printed and bound by Quebecor/Dubuque.

This book is printed on recycled, acid-free paper containing a minimum of 50% recycled, de-inked fiber.

Contents

Hi, I am Doctor Heidi.
I am going to show you some amazing experiments about light and color.
My *Little Scientists*® friend, Olivia, loves exploring.
Together we will discover how light creates the colors in a rainbow.

Why is it dark outside?

Do you ever wonder why you don't see the sun shine on cloudy days? This experiment will show you how clouds can affect light.

You will need
- 1 sheet of white paper
- Table
- Flashlight
- A room that can be darkened
- Ruler
- 1 sheet of clear plastic (report covers work well)
- 1 sheet of black construction paper
- Large square of wax paper (12" x 12")

1. Place the sheet of white paper on a table. Darken the room. Turn on the flashlight and hold it 12 inches above the white paper.

2. Hold the clear plastic 3 inches below the light. Does the light on the white paper look different?

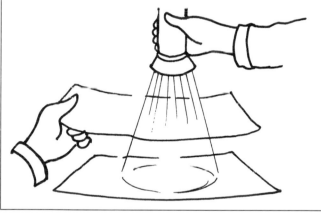

3. Replace the clear plastic with the wax paper. Does the light look different now?

4. Replace the wax paper with the sheet of black paper. What do you see?

Did you notice how the light looked when you shined it through the clear plastic? Through the wax paper? Through the black paper?

The plastic is **transparent**. It lets the light through, just as air lets sunlight reach us.

The wax paper is **translucent** and scatters the light, just as clouds scatter the sunlight before it reaches us.

The black construction paper is **opaque** and blocks the light, just as walls and curtains can keep out sunlight.

Why does the straw
look broken?

When light moves through water, it slows down and bends,
causing objects to look larger than they really are. This is called **refraction**.
See how refraction works in this next experiment.

You will *need*
- Short clear drinking glass
- Long pencil
- Water

1. Fill the glass with water.

2. Put the pencil in the glass of water. Make sure that half of the pencil is out of the water.

3. Now look at the glass at eye level. What does the pencil look like outside of the water?

How does it look different from the part of the pencil in the water?

The pencil beneath the water looks thicker and
appears detached from the top half of the pencil.
The water **refracts** the light and changes how the pencil looks.

What makes these straws look different?

This experiment will show you how light bends in water.

You will need
- Safety scissors
- Ruler
- Cardboard shoebox
- 1 sheet of white paper
- Clear drinking glass
- Water
- Flashlight
- A room that can be darkened
- Pencil

1. Using the scissors cut two narrow vertical slits, 1 inch apart, at the front end of the cardboard shoebox.

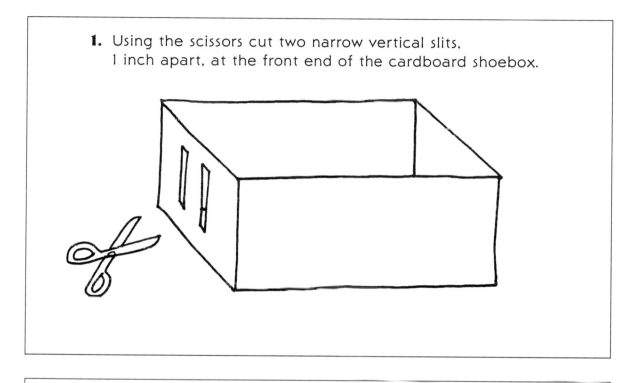

2. Put the white paper on the inside bottom of the box. Place the paper on the end opposite from the slits.

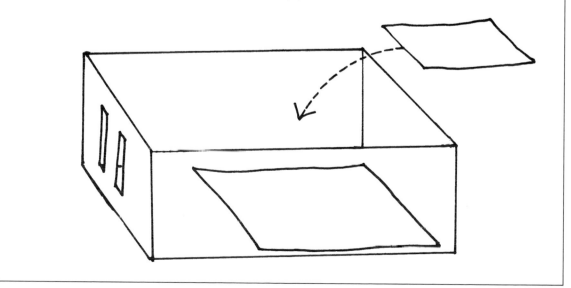

Continued on the next page.

3. Fill the glass with water and place it in the middle of the shoebox, on top of the white paper.

4. Darken the room and turn on the flashlight.

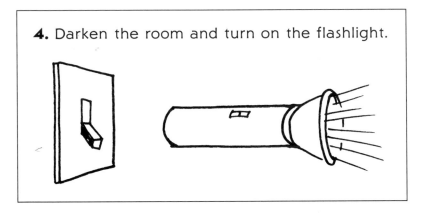

5. Hold the flashlight several inches away from the shoebox. Aim the light so it shines through the vertical slits and into the water in the glass. Do you see the light bending?

Continued on the next page.

6. Mark with a pencil where the beams of light cross each other.
Do you see the two separate beams of light on the back of the box?

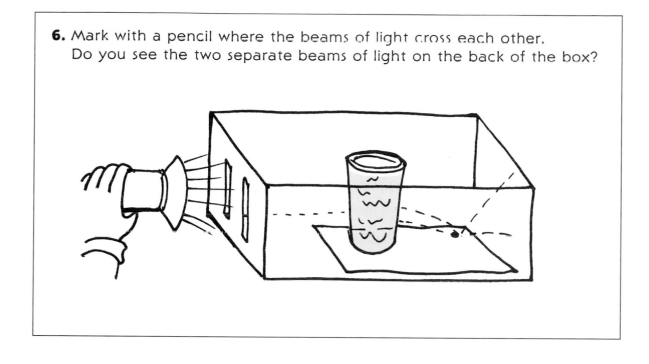

7. Move the flashlight farther away from the slits.
Do you see a difference in the bending light?

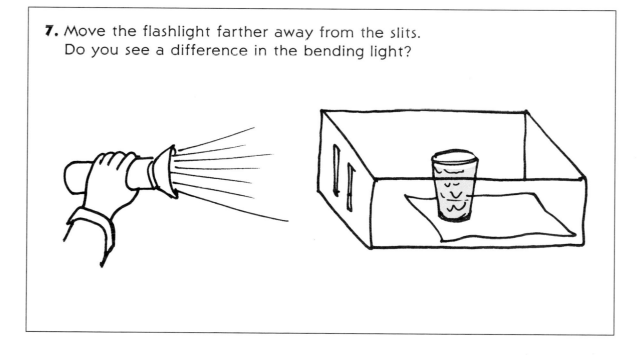

Where do the colors
in a rainbow come from?

Sunlight looks white, but it is actually made up of the seven colors in a rainbow.
Try this experiment to find the rainbow in white light!

You will *need*
- Clear plastic container
- Mirror that can fit in the container
- Small stone, or object that supports the mirror at a 45-degree angle
- Water
- A room that can be darkened
- Ruler
- Flashlight
- 1 sheet of white paper

1. Position the mirror in the container, with the small stone or object supporting it at a 45-degree angle.

2. Fill the container with water.

3. Darken the room and turn on your flashlight.

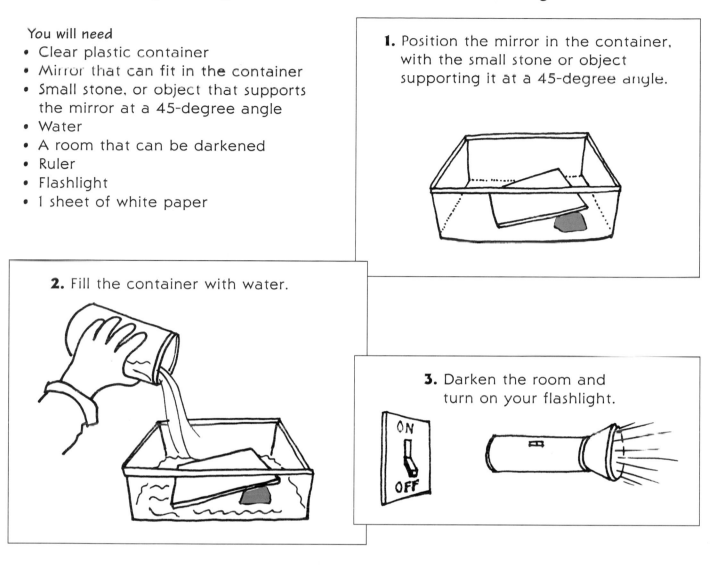

4. With one hand hold the paper 12 inches above the water, and facing the mirror. With your other hand, point the flashlight down into the water at the mirror. The light should reflect off the mirror onto the white paper. Move the flashlight until you see the reflection of the rainbow on the paper.

How can water
make a rainbow?

Small droplets of water that are in the sky bend sunlight, creating a rainbow.
Let's do an experiment to see how!

You will need
- Sunshine
- Assistance from an adult friend
- Garden hose attached to an outside water faucet

1. Hold the spray nozzle and stand with the sun behind you.

2. Have your friend turn on the faucet of the garden hose.

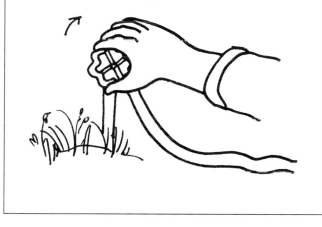

3. Spray water into the air in front of you, moving the hose back and forth in a wide arc. If necessary, turn the hose a little to the left or to the right. You should be able to create your own rainbow right in your yard!

How can I make a rainbow?

You can make a rainbow using a drinking glass.
Try this experiment to find out how!

You will need
- Sunshine
- Thick clear drinking glass
- White bed sheet
- Yardstick or ruler
- Windowsill or table next to a sunny window

1. On a sunny day, place the drinking glass next to a sunlit windowsill.

2. Position the sheet 5 to 10 feet away from the window.

5–10 feet

When the sun is shining through the glass, look at the sheet for any rainbows.

You can try this experiment using different objects on the windowsill.
White light bends when passing through clear glass and can produce
all of the colors of a rainbow.

How can my glass charm make a rainbow?

Raindrops or glass prisms form rainbows by bending white light.
The colors of the rainbow are always the same and always in this order:
red, orange, yellow, green, blue, indigo, and violet.
You can use the **acronym ROY G BIV** to remember these colors!
Find out how water can bend white light into all of the colors of a rainbow
by trying this experiment.

You will need
- Safety scissors
- Black construction paper (6" x 4")
- Tape
- Tall drinking glass
- 1 sheet of white paper
- Water
- A room that can be darkened
- Flashlight

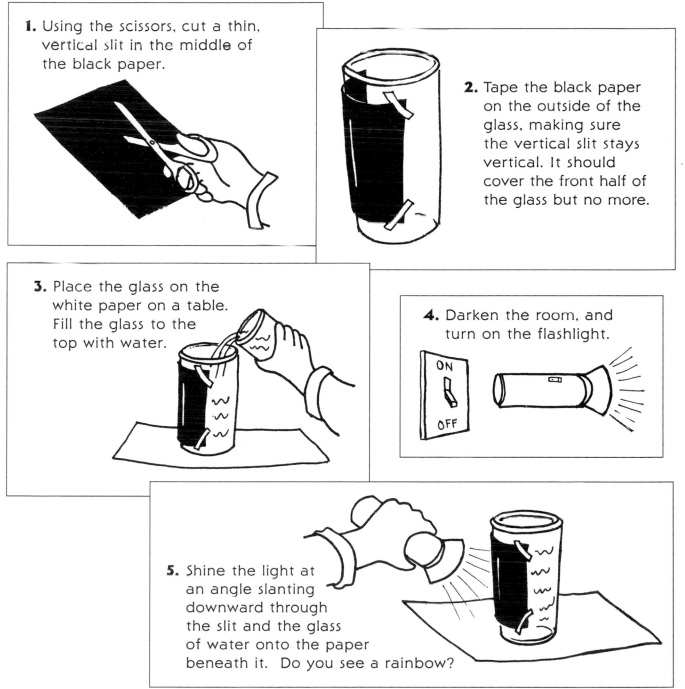

1. Using the scissors, cut a thin, vertical slit in the middle of the black paper.

2. Tape the black paper on the outside of the glass, making sure the vertical slit stays vertical. It should cover the front half of the glass but no more.

3. Place the glass on the white paper on a table. Fill the glass to the top with water.

4. Darken the room, and turn on the flashlight.

5. Shine the light at an angle slanting downward through the slit and the glass of water onto the paper beneath it. Do you see a rainbow?

Why is the sky blue and not green?

Try this experiment to find out why the sky is blue.

You will need
- 2 32-ounce plastic, clear containers (large deli containers)
- 1 sheet of white paper
- Water
- Spoon
- Powdered milk (1/8 teaspoon)
- A room that can be darkened
- Flashlight
- 1/8 teaspoon
- Measuring cup
- Ruler

1. Place the two containers on a sheet of white paper. Fill each container with 3 cups of water.

2. Darken the room, and turn on the flashlight. Shine the light into the top of each container. What color do you see looking through the side of the containers?

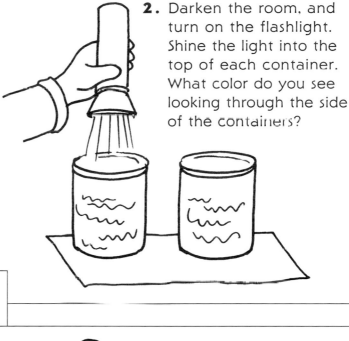

3. Add 1/8 of a teaspoon of powdered milk to the water in one container. Stir it. What do you see?

4. Hold the flashlight 12 inches above the water and shine the light into each container.

12 inches

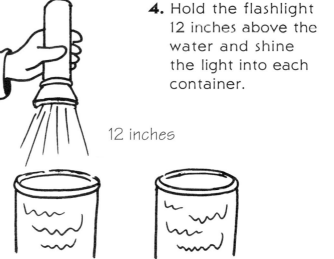

The light you can see in the plain water is clear and colorless while the light you see in the container with water and milk looks blue. The light we see from the sun looks white. However, we have learned that light is made up of a **spectrum** of colors. Water droplets, dust, and dirt in the sky scatter the white light from the sun, making only the blue color visible to us.

Why do letters
look backwards
in a mirror?

When you look in a mirror, you are seeing a **reflection** of yourself.
However, the image is actually reversed.

You will need
- Crayons
- Several sheets of white paper
- Small mirror
- The maze on the next page
- Coloring book
- Table

1. Write your name on a piece of paper with a crayon.

2. Hold it in front of the mirror, with the writing facing the mirror. What do the letters look like? Can you read it?

3. Choose a page from the coloring book and put it on a table in front of you. Hold the mirror facing you so that you can see the page when you look in the mirror.

4. Try to color the picture when you are only looking in the mirror. DON'T peek at the page!

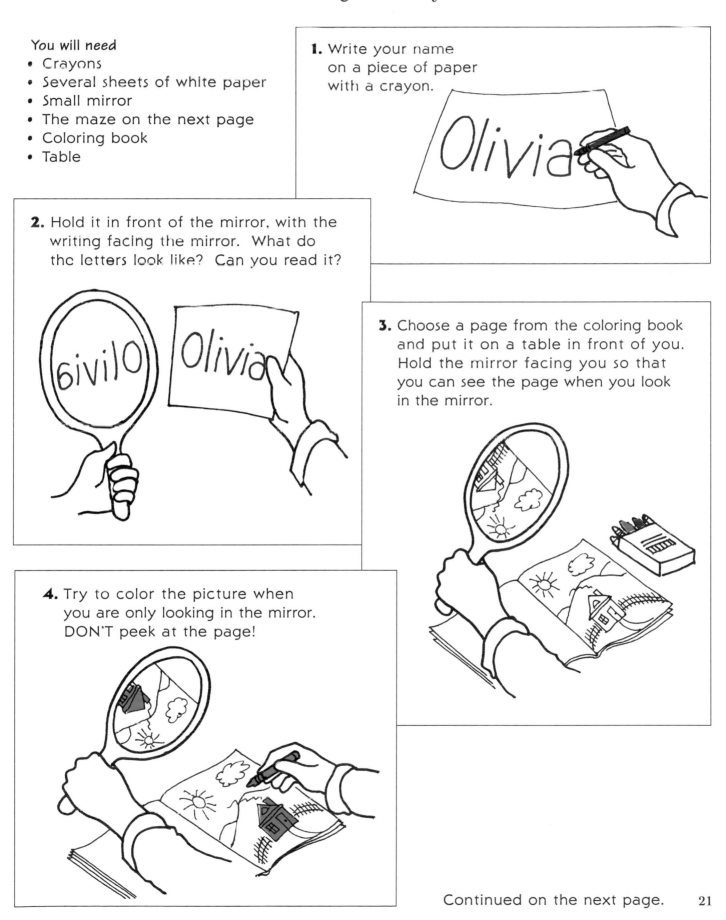

Continued on the next page.

5. Put the mirror in front of the maze on this page,
just like you did with the coloring book. Use your finger
to get through the maze without touching the lines
and without looking at your hand or the page.

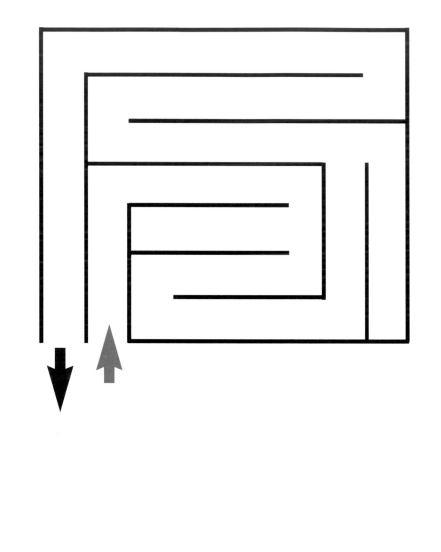

Were you able to make it through without peeking?

Continued on the next page.

6. Place the mirror just above the word MOM shown on this page. What can you read in the mirror?

MOM

How do mirrors work?

If you use two mirrors, you can increase the number of pictures you see.
Try out this experiment.

1. Hold the mirrors facing one another and touching on one edge at a right angle (90 degrees).

You will need
• 2 small mirrors
• Small toy or object

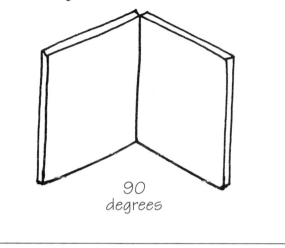

90 degrees

2. Stand your toy between the mirrors, facing one of them. How many images do you see? (You should be able to see three images. If not, look again!)

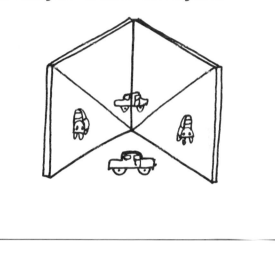

3. Move the open edges of the mirrors closer together (60 degrees). Now how many images do you see? Do you see more or fewer images than before? (You should be able to see six. If not, look again!)

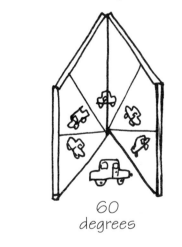

60 degrees

4. Hold the mirrors facing one another (parallel). Place your toy in between the two mirrors. Peek over the edge of one of the mirrors and look at the other mirror. How many images do you see now? Are there more images? (The images should go on and on. You cannot count them all!)

If you hold two mirrors facing each other, you can see infinite (never-ending) images. Light reflects off of one mirror and then off of the other mirror over and over.

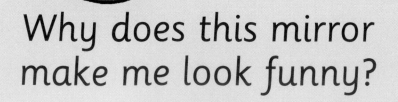

Why does this mirror
make me look funny?

26

When you look in a flat mirror, you see a reflection of yourself and what is around you. Though the images are backwards, they look very much like they do in real life. This is not what you see when you look in a curved mirror. Find out what you see in a curved mirror by trying this experiment.

You will need
- Large, shiny, metal spoon
  (a new spoon works best)

1. Look at the back of your spoon. You can see yourself, but what do you look like?

CONVEX

2. Look at the other side of the spoon. Can you see yourself? How do you look? Is this really what you look like?

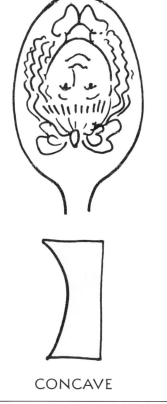

CONCAVE

Go on an adventure!
Look around your house for shiny objects in which you can see yourself, like pans, lids, and doorknobs.
Is the reflection upside-down or right side up?

Curved mirrors distort or change your image.
If it is curved outward, like the back of the spoon, it is called **convex**.
If it is curved inward, like the inside of the spoon, it is called **concave**.
A concave reflection is upside-down!

How does this mirror let me see what is down the other aisle?

Mirrors can be helpful in many ways.
You can use mirrors to see around corners.
Your dentist uses a mirror to see in your mouth to clean your teeth.
Cars have mirrors so drivers can see what is happening behind them.
In the next experiment, you can use a mirror to try to see hidden things!

You will need
- Hand-held mirror
- Small object or toy

1. Find a corner of the hallway or doorway in your house. Put your small toy on one side of the corner.

2. Stand on the other side of the corner. Use your mirror to see what is around the corner.

3. Hold the mirror different ways to find your toy on the other side. You will need to hold it facing you and out a little around the corner. You might have to squat down or stand up tall. Keep trying until you see your toy!

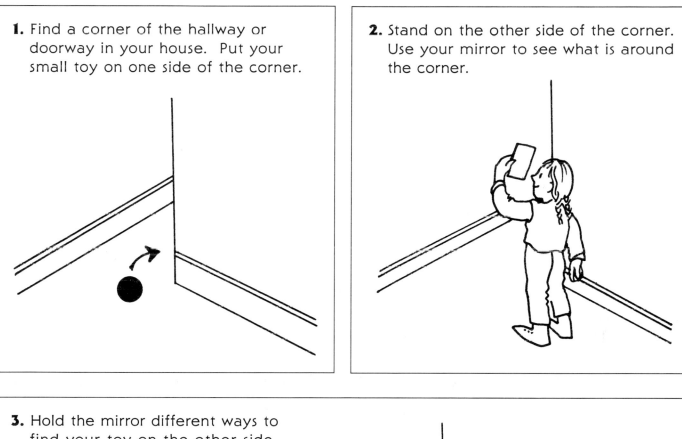

What makes a shadow?

Some objects are **opaque**, which means the object blocks light.
Some objects are **transparent**, which means they let light through.
Objects that are opaque have shadows.
Objects that are transparent do not have shadows.

You will *need*
- Table
- Clear unbreakable drinking glass
- Sheet of plastic wrap
- Crayon

- 3 small toys or objects
- A room that can be darkened
- Flashlight
- Light-colored bare wall

1. Place each of the objects on the table. Separate the drinking glass, plastic wrap, crayon, and three of your favorite small objects into two groups. Put the objects that you think will make a shadow in one group. Put the objects that you think will not make a shadow in the other group.

2. Darken the room and turn on the flashlight.

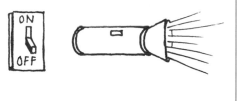

3. Choose one of the objects and hold it a few feet away from the wall. Shine the flashlight straight at the object. Do you see a shadow on the wall or does the light shine through the object?

One by one, shine the flashlight on the rest of the objects. As you test each object, place each one in the correct group: opaque or transparent.

Did you guess correctly?
If the object was opaque, it made a shadow.
No light went through it.
The object blocked the light and you saw a **shadow**.

What makes some shadows look so big?

In the next experiment, we will have more fun playing with shadows!
(We'll also find out why some shadows are bigger than others.)

You will need
- A room that can be darkened
- Flashlight
- Table near a wall
- Several toys

1. Make the room dark and turn on the flashlight. Rest the flashlight on the table so that it is shining at the wall.

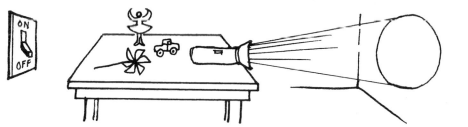

2. Choose a toy and hold it in the beam of light. Move the toy closer to the flashlight and then closer to the wall. How are the shadows different?

3. The closer the object is to the flashlight, the larger the shadow will appear on the wall. Is the shadow fuzzy or clear? Does it look like the object?

4. The closer the object is to the wall, the smaller the shadow will appear on the wall. What does the shadow look like now? Repeat steps 2 – 4 with each toy.

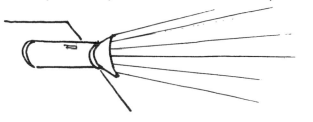

A shadow also changes when you move the light that is shining on an object.
If you move the light farther away from the object, its shadow grows smaller.
If you move the light closer to the object, its shadow is bigger.

Why does my shadow always follow me?

Have you ever taken a close look at your shadow?
In the next experiment, you will be able to see if
you can separate yourself from your shadow.

1. Stand outside with the sun behind you.
Make sure you are standing with an
area of flat ground in front of you.
Try to find a way to make your shadow
look like it is not attached to you.

You will **need**
- Sunshine
- Large area of flat ground

2. Stand on one foot.
Is it still attached?

3. Sit down. Is it still attached?
Try other things to disconnect
your shadow. Did you find a way?

4. Now jump in the air. Is your shadow
still attached to you? You should be
able to see it separate!

A shadow happens when
an object blocks light.
When you see the outline
of that object, you are
seeing its shadow.

35

How many colors can I see?

Our eyes can see more than 300,000 colors. Let's do an experiment
to see how many different kinds of blue you can find in your room.

1. Look around your room to see
how many blue items you have.

You will *need*
- Items in your room
- Color wheel

2. Put all of the blue items
in a pile on the floor.

3. Put them in order to match the color wheel
from greenish-blue to bluish-purple.

4. Put them in order from lightest to darkest.

Red, yellow, and blue are the **primary colors**.
In our next experiment, we will figure out what is so special about these three colors.

1. Look around your house to find five red, five yellow, and five blue objects.

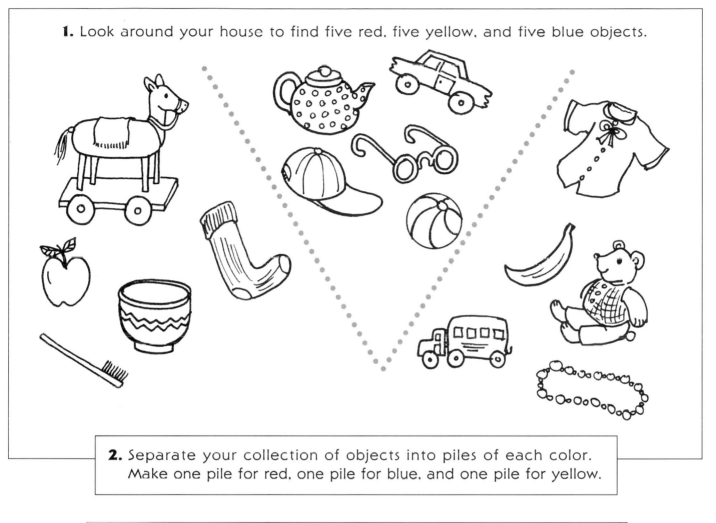

2. Separate your collection of objects into piles of each color.
Make one pile for red, one pile for blue, and one pile for yellow.

3. What does each color make you think of?

How do I make another color,
like purple?

Do you know how to make new colors
using only the primary colors red, yellow, and blue?
Mixing two primary colors together makes a secondary color.
Let's paint all the colors of the rainbow, using these three primary colors as a starting point!

You will need
- Pencil
- White construction paper
- Paint brushes or cotton swabs
- Red, yellow, and blue paints

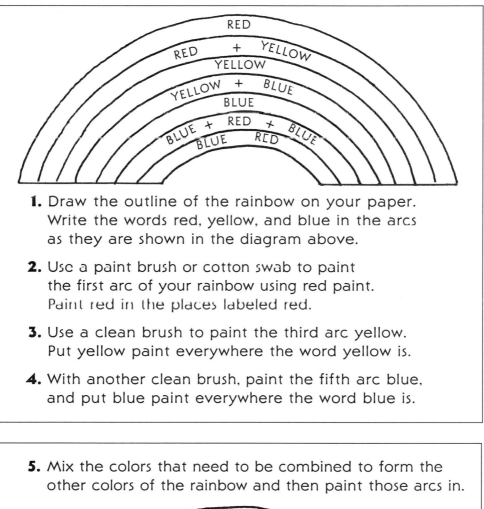

1. Draw the outline of the rainbow on your paper.
   Write the words red, yellow, and blue in the arcs
   as they are shown in the diagram above.

2. Use a paint brush or cotton swab to paint
   the first arc of your rainbow using red paint.
   Paint red in the places labeled red.

3. Use a clean brush to paint the third arc yellow.
   Put yellow paint everywhere the word yellow is.

4. With another clean brush, paint the fifth arc blue,
   and put blue paint everywhere the word blue is.

5. Mix the colors that need to be combined to form the
   other colors of the rainbow and then paint those arcs in.

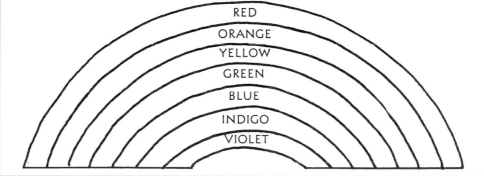

Rainbows have all of the primary and secondary colors.
There are seven colors in a rainbow. The sixth color is indigo,
which is between blue and violet. Violet is another name for purple.

41

When I add white to red, I change the color to pink. I wonder if white does anything to the other colors?

There are primary colors, secondary colors, and **shades** of colors. Adding white to a color makes lighter shades of that color. Pink is a lighter shade of red. In this activity, you will make several shades of your favorite color.

1. Use the pencil to number each strip of paper 1 through 7.

You will need
- Pencil
- 7 strips of white paper (2" x 5")
- Paint brush
- 2 tablespoons
- Bowl of your favorite color paint (anything but white)
- Large plate for mixing colors
- Cup of white paint

2. Take the brush and paint the first paper strip with your favorite color.

3. With the tablespoon, place one spoonful of the colored paint on the plate.

4. Using the other spoon, add three small drops of the white paint to the colored paint.

5. Mix the two paints together with the paint brush. What happened? You just made a lighter shade of your favorite color.

Paint the second paper strip with the new color you just made. Make sure to keep the painted strips of paper in order.

6. Repeat steps 4 and 5. Continue to add an additional three drops of white paint as you fill in the remainder of the paper strips. Now you have seven different shades of one color. Can you see the gradual change in color? Once the paint is dry, mix up the order of the paint strips. Can you put them back in order without looking at the numbers?

Why is the picture changing colors?

44

When you look at a watercolor marker, you see one color.
In fact, most markers are made up of more than one color.
The science of separating colors is called **chromatography**.
In the next experiment, we will separate the colors in a watercolor marker!

You will need
- Ruler
- Safety scissors
- Coffee filters
- Watercolor markers (brown, black, and purple will work best)
- 8-ounce paper or plastic cup
- Tablespoon
- Water

1. Cut a strip one-inch wide and halfway across a coffee filter. Do not cut the strip off — leave it attached in the middle.

2. Fold the strip so it hangs down. Using a brown marker, draw a spot on the strip 2 inches from the end.

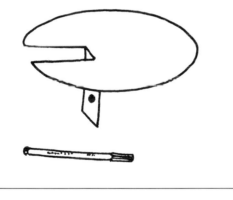

3. Put one tablespoon of water into the cup. Cover the top of the cup with the filter, making sure the strip falls inside and the edge just touches the water.

4. Watch as the coffee filter soaks up the water. Watch the spot of color as the water moves to it. What is happening? Can you see the brown separating into colors such as green, red, and yellow?

Repeat the entire experiment, using the black and purple markers to make spots on clean filters. Try other colors, too. What colors separate more easily than other colors?

Why is it hard to see color
in the dark?

Your eyes need a lot of light to work correctly, so it is hard to see colors at night. In the next experiment, we will discover that some colors show up better in the dark.

You will need
- Shoebox with lid
- Assistance from an adult friend
- Safety scissors
- Ruler
- 2-inch square pieces of colored paper (red, yellow, orange, blue, black, and white)
- Glue stick or tape
- Flashlight
- Black construction paper
- 6 drinking straws
- A room that can be darkened

1. Remove the lid from the shoebox. With help from a friend, cut off one end of the box. Near the other end of the box, cut a slot on the long side that is 2 ½ inches high and ½ inch wide.

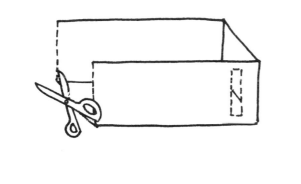

2. Line the inside of the box and the lid with black construction paper, using glue or tape. Don't cover the slot you just cut! Replace the lid on the box.

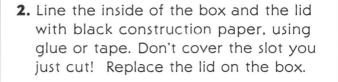

3. Tape a piece of each different colored paper onto the end of each straw.

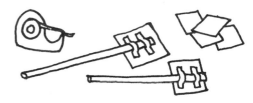

4. Darken the room and turn the flashlight on. Hold the flashlight 12 inches away from the box and shine it into the opening. Insert the straw with the black paper into the slot in the box. What do you see? Repeat this with each different color. Insert the blue paper into the box. Is the blue easier to see than the black? Insert the yellow paper into the slot. What do you see?

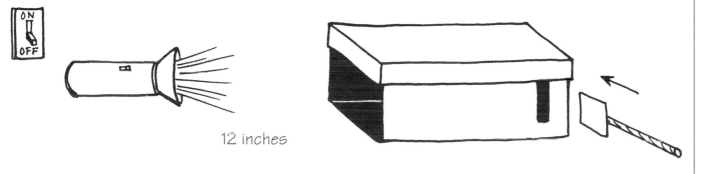

12 inches

Based on what you just learned, what colors do you think are easier to see at night?

Why is the black toy hotter than the white one?

Sunlight is the energy that heats the Earth.
The color white **reflects** heat and light, while the color black **absorbs** heat and light.
We can prove this fact in our next experiment!

You will need
- 2 clear unbreakable cups
- Tape
- Black construction paper
- Safety scissors
- White construction paper
- Measuring cup
- Cool water
- A sunny window
- Clock or timer

1. Tape black construction paper around the outside of one clear cup. Cut off the excess. Save enough black paper to cover the top, but do not cover it yet!

Tape white construction paper around the other cup and cut off the excess. Save enough white paper to cover the top.

2. Pour 1 cup of cool (not cold) water into each cup.

3. Set the cups on a sunny windowsill. Cover the white cup with the leftover white paper and the black cup with the black paper.

4. Let the cups sit in the sunshine for about four hours. What do you think will happen?

The water in the black cup should be warmer than the water in the white cup.

You should be able to feel the difference with your finger!

This proves that white reflects heat and black absorbs heat. It also explains why you should wear white clothing in the summertime to keep yourself cooler!

Why does the sky
change colors when
the sun goes down?

When the sun sets, it is shining light at the Earth at a different angle and through larger particles in the sky, so we see only the orange and red colors of the sunlight! Try this experiment and see for yourself.

You will need
- Sheet of white paper
- 2 32-ounce plastic, clear containers
- Measuring cup
- 6 cups of water
- Flashlight
- Teaspoon
- Dry powdered milk (1 teaspoon)

1. Place the containers on a sheet of white paper. Fill each container with 3 cups of water.

2. Shine the flashlight into the side of one container. What color do you see on the white paper?

Continued on the next page.

3. Add ¹/₂ teaspoon of dry powdered milk to the water in one container.

4. Stir with a spoon to dissolve it.

5. Shine the flashlight through the container from the side. What color do you see on the white paper?

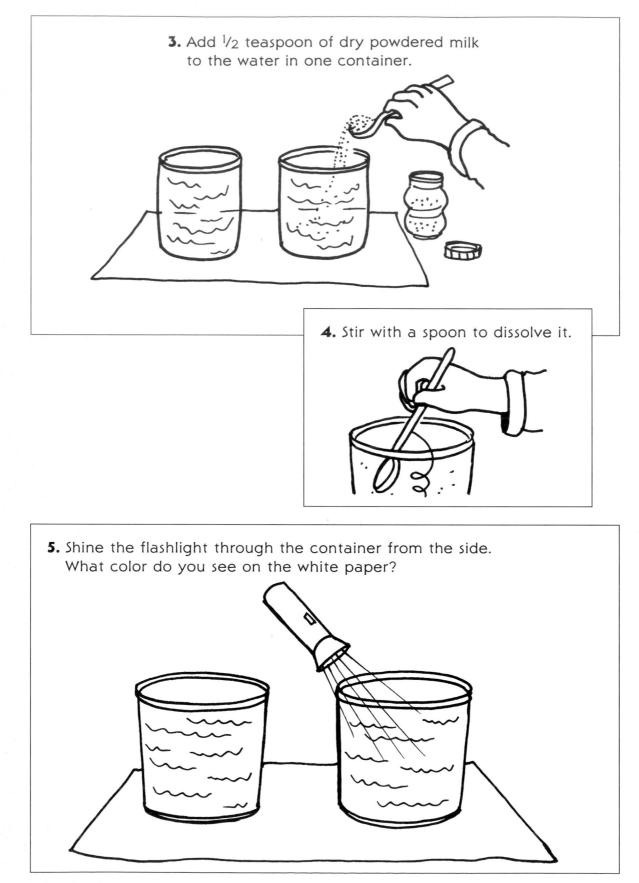

Continued on the next page.

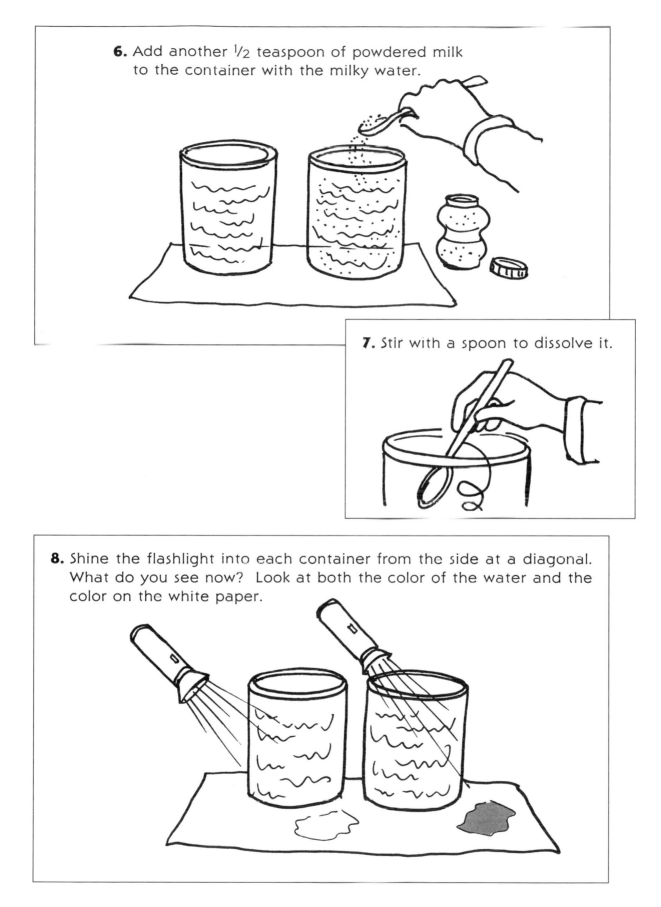

6. Add another ¹/₂ teaspoon of powdered milk to the container with the milky water.

7. Stir with a spoon to dissolve it.

8. Shine the flashlight into each container from the side at a diagonal. What do you see now? Look at both the color of the water and the color on the white paper.

The water in the container with the milk will look blue,
while the light coming out of that container will look red, like the sunset.

How does a kaleidoscope work?

Have you ever looked through a **kaleidoscope**?
A kaleidoscope uses mirrors and light to form beautiful patterns.
Light passes through the tube of the kaleidoscope and the object chamber.
The colorful objects appear to be multiplied by the mirrors, which are set at angles
to each other, making beautiful patterns. As the tube is turned, the image
will change because the objects can move inside the object chamber.

You will *need*
- Ruler
- Cardboard paper towel tube
- Safety scissors
- Things to decorate the outside of the tube
  (such as crayons, stickers, glue, or construction paper)
- Pencil
- 1 sheet of cardboard (8 ½" x 11")
- Black construction paper
- Clear, hard plastic report cover
  (available at an office supply store)
- Tape
- Clear plastic wrap
- 3 rubber bands
- Wax paper
- 6 or 7 small objects for the viewing chamber
  (such as small beads, sequins, or cut up feathers)

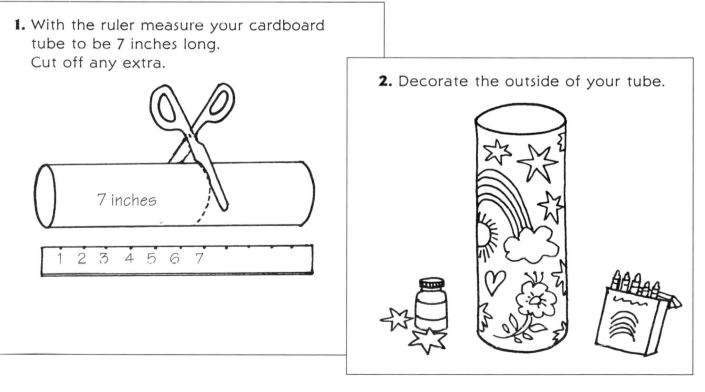

1. With the ruler measure your cardboard
tube to be 7 inches long.
Cut off any extra.

7 inches

1 2 3 4 5 6 7

2. Decorate the outside of your tube.

Continued on the next page.

3. With the pencil trace the rectangle shape shown below, three times onto a sheet of cardboard. Cut out the pieces. Repeat this step with black construction paper and hard plastic. You should have nine rectangular pieces exactly the same size.

7 inches

1 inch

4. Make a sandwich as follows:
- hard plastic on the bottom
- black paper in the middle
- cardboard on top

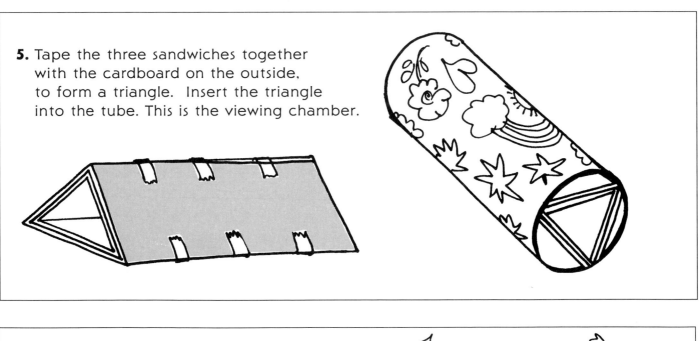

cardboard

black paper

plastic

Make two more sandwiches exactly the same way, for a total of three sandwiches.

5. Tape the three sandwiches together with the cardboard on the outside, to form a triangle. Insert the triangle into the tube. This is the viewing chamber.

6. Cover each end of the tube with a piece of plastic wrap. Secure the plastic tightly in place with a rubber band.

Continued on the next page.

7. Place six or seven small objects (such as sequins or beads) on top of the plastic wrap at one end of the tube.

Loosely cover the objects with the wax paper. Secure the wax paper around the tube with the rubber band.

8. Look through the other end of the kaleidoscope. What do you see? Turn the tube to see the images change.

Take off the wax paper and try other materials in the object chamber. What happens when you put too many things in the object chamber?

Although this is the last experiment in this book, don't let it be your last experiment. Keep observing what is happening around you. Test things out by doing your own experiments. Maybe you'll even discover something new!

Glossary

chromatography — a process that separates a mixed color into its individual parts

concave — curving inward

convex — curving outward

opaque — not letting light through

pigments — substances which produce one or more colors

primary colors — red, yellow, and blue (for reflected light) or red, green, and blue (for direct light)

prism — a clear object which scatters light to produce a continuous rainbow

reflection — the bouncing of light or an image off the surface of certain materials (glass, metal, etc.)

refraction — how light bends as it passes from one material (such as air, water, or glass) into another

ROY G BIV — an acronym for **R**ed, **O**range, **Y**ellow, **G**reen, **B**lue, **I**ndigo, and **V**iolet — the colors of the rainbow

secondary colors — colors which are produced by combining two primary colors

shades — variations of a color which are either darker or lighter

shadow — a dark area produced by an object blocking light

spectrum — a continuous rainbow

translucent — letting light through, but not clearly

transparent — letting light through clearly